THIS BOOK BELONGS TO:

_____

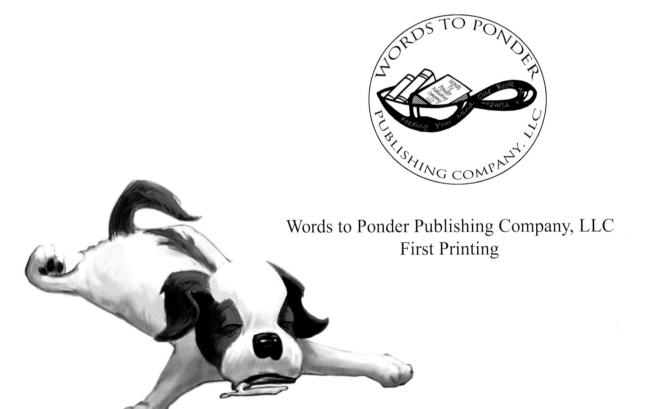

Words to Ponder Publishing Company, LLC
First Printing

For Trefus, my soulmate,
Jessica and Melissa, my pride and joy, and
Michael R. Brumage, my mentor and friend.

Thank you! - F.D.L.

In our lives, we oftentimes have people who come to us
when we need them the most...when we are "chasing
our tails". These are the ones who help guide and shape
us into who we really are. I want to dedicate this book
to all of them: friends and family alike.

Thank you, - M.W.

Forward

How much of our lives do we end up chasing our tails? Like Max, we are caught up in habits that hurt us without even remembering why we started in the first place. Days, weeks, months, and even many years go by without the awareness of our habits.

Perhaps we can teach our children something better by becoming aware of their breath and aware of their behaviors, just like Ross teaches Max in Florenza Denise Lee's wonderful story, The Tail of Max the Mindless Dog.

Denise has created a mindful story to teach our children about how we can break habitual, non-productive behaviors by riding the wave of the breath. And just maybe the adults or older children who read this book aloud to the younger children will learn something, too!

Thank you Denise, for following your vision.

Michael R. Brumage, MD,
MPH Camp Zama, Japan
January 2015

THE TAIL OF MAX THE Mindless DOG

A CHILDREN'S BOOK ON MINDFULNESS

WORDS TO PONDER PUBLISHING COMPANY, LLC
Feeding Your Mind One Book At A Time™

Written by: Florenza Lee   *Illustrated by: Michelle Wynn*

Meet Max

As a puppy, Max's tail would oftentimes get hurt. No matter how hard he would try, something would happen to cause him pain.

As he slept, it would hurt. While he was eating, it would hurt.

Even if Max was doing absolutely nothing at all, something would happen to his tail and he would find himself yelping in pain.

As Max grew older, he thought his tail was the source of his pain. One day he said to himself, "I'm going to catch my tail and tie it in a knot so it will never get hurt again!"

He went around and around in circles trying to catch his tail.
Max went around so fast, that he soon became dizzy.

Panting for air, Max declared,
"I'm going to catch you yet, tail."

Then poor
Max plopped
down and
took a nap.

As soon as he woke up, he found that his tail was hurting again, so he ran around and around in circles...trying to catch his tail.

Day after day, Max would chase his tail. After a while, he forgot why he was even running in circles and thought it was what he was supposed to be doing.

Max chased his tail while at ballgames and missed all the innings. During recess, he chased his tail while the other students were running, skipping, and playing games.

His friends would invite him to come over and have fun, but before he could reach them, he found himself running around in circles.

After a while, his friends began to call
him Max, the Mindless Dog because
he seemed to have only one thing on his
mind: catching his tail.

His friends shook their heads and said,
"Poor Max, doesn't he know he will never catch his tail?"

One day, Max's friend, Ross asked him, "Hey, Max, why do you always chase your tail?" Max paused, but realized that he did not have an answer; he had been chasing his tail for so long, he had forgotten why he was chasing it in the first place.

Max replied, "I don't know, I guess it is a habit."

Then Max continued to run in circles.

Max Learns a New Habit

Days later, Ross was walking by and saw his friend frantically running in circles and said to himself, "Max is missing out on all the fun in life. I have to help my friend. I know just what to do. I am going to help him learn a new habit."

Ross walked up to Max, tapped him on the shoulder, and said, "Max, today you will learn a new habit. You will learn to spend your time having fun." Max was so happy he began to bounce up and down. He had always wanted to have fun but didn't know how. Max asked his friend how he was going to learn a new habit.

Breathe In and Out

Ross said, "If you find yourself chasing your tail, I want you to stop, close your eyes and concentrate on the feeling of the air as it enters your nose and leaves.

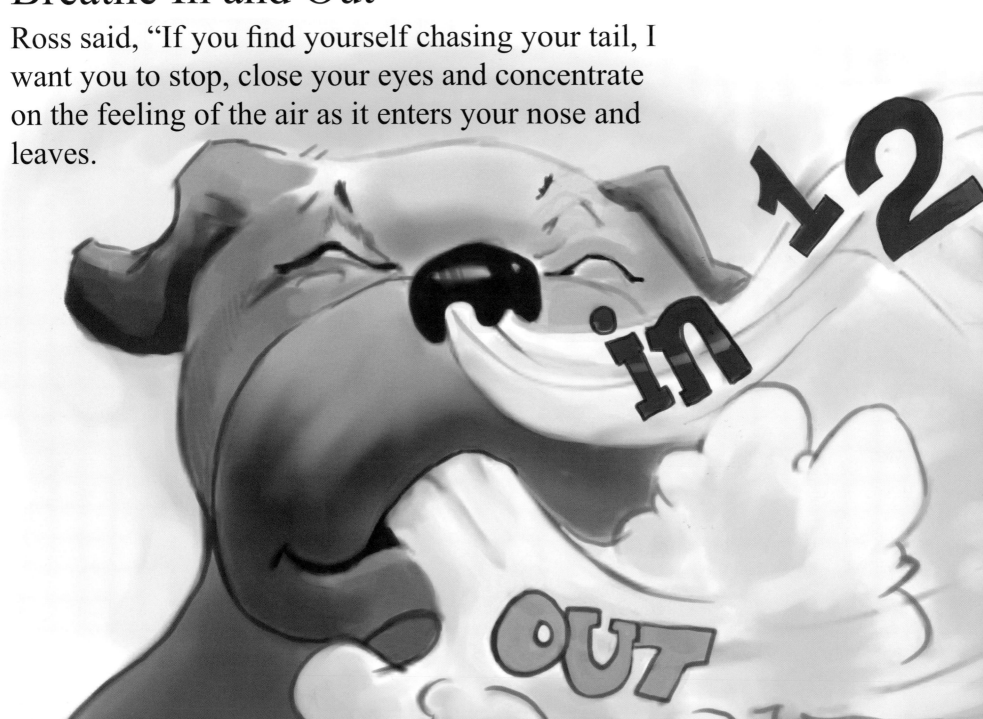

As you are breathing, say 'in' for each breath in and 'out' for each breath out. When you count to ten breaths in and ten out, repeat these words:

"I will not chase my tail today.
I will not chase it any day.
I'll use my time for friends and fun,
to hop and skip and play and run.
I will not waste another day.
I'd rather use my time to play."

Itchy Twitchy

Max was almost home when all of the sudden,

his nose started to twitch and his tail started to wiggle, and he found himself chasing his tail. "Oh, no," said Max, "I am chasing my tail again."

He then remembered the wise words of his friend, Ross.

Max stopped, closed his eyes, and breathed in
and out, counting his breaths until he reached
the number ten. Then he said,

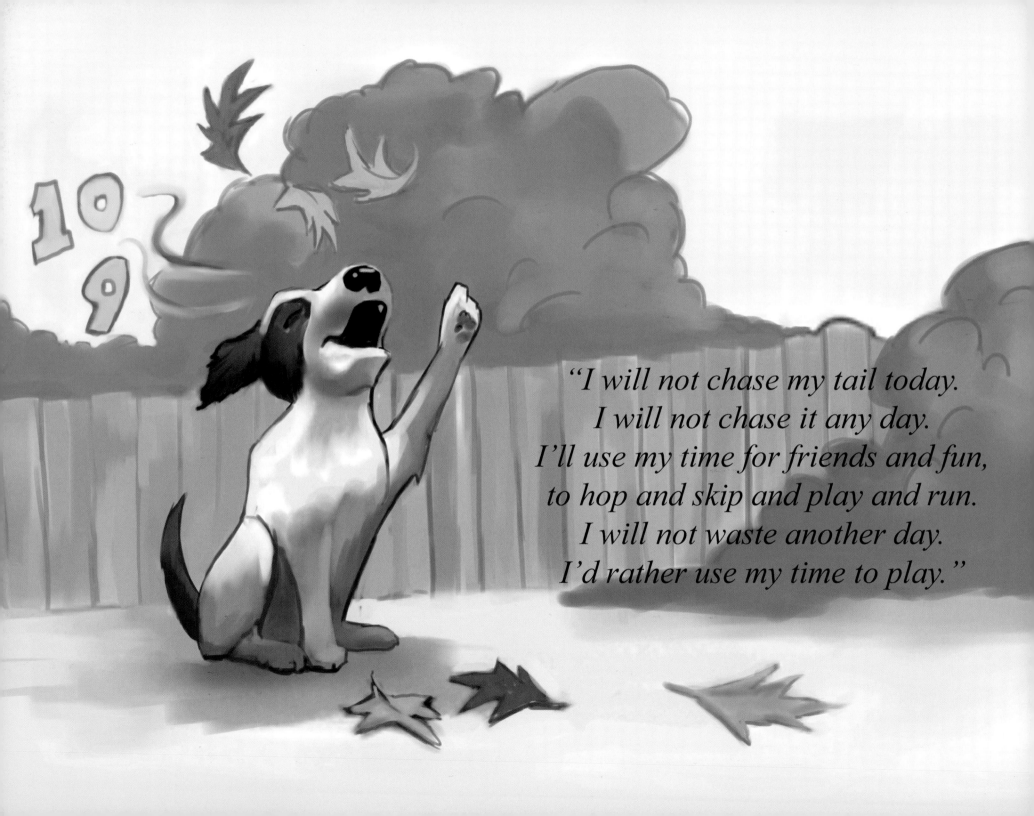

Championship Game

When Max opened his eyes, he was happy to see that he was not frantically chasing his tail but had become...very calm.

He could not believe it. Counting his breaths in and out and then saying the words Ross had taught him had helped. Just then, his friends were walking down the street going to play baseball.

Olivia said to Lauren, "Hey, there's Max. We need one more player for the game; can't he play on our team?"

Lauren said, "Yes, we need another player but Max always chases his tail. He could never play baseball and this is our championship game."

As Lauren was speaking, Olivia looked and noticed that Max was not chasing his tail at all!

He was just standing there smiling. "Hey, Max," said Olivia, "Do you want to play baseball with us? We need another player for our championship game."

Home Run

He was so happy; he said yes right away and ran over to be with them. Max was so good at baseball, he hit the home run that allowed his team to win the championship game.

Everyone cheered for him.

Lauren asked Max how he learned not to chase his tail. He smiled and said, "Each time I feel like chasing my tail, I stop, close my eyes and concentrate breathing in and breathing out, then I say 'in' for each breath in and 'out' for each breath out.

After I count ten breaths in and out, I say,

"I will not chase my tail today.
I will not chase it any day.
I'll use my time for friends and fun,
to hop and skip and play and run.
I will not waste another day.
I'd rather use my time to play."

His friends put him on their shoulders, and cheered aloud, "We are so happy for you, Max, we are going to change your name to Mindful Max.

Mindful Max

Many years passed and Mindful Max became old and gray.

As he was walking down the road,
he saw a little puppy chasing his tail.
He remembered the days when he used to do the same,
so he walked over to the pup and said...

"Son, whenever you feel like you need to chase your tail, I want you to stop, close your eyes, and concentrate on the feeling of the air as it enters your nose and as it leaves."

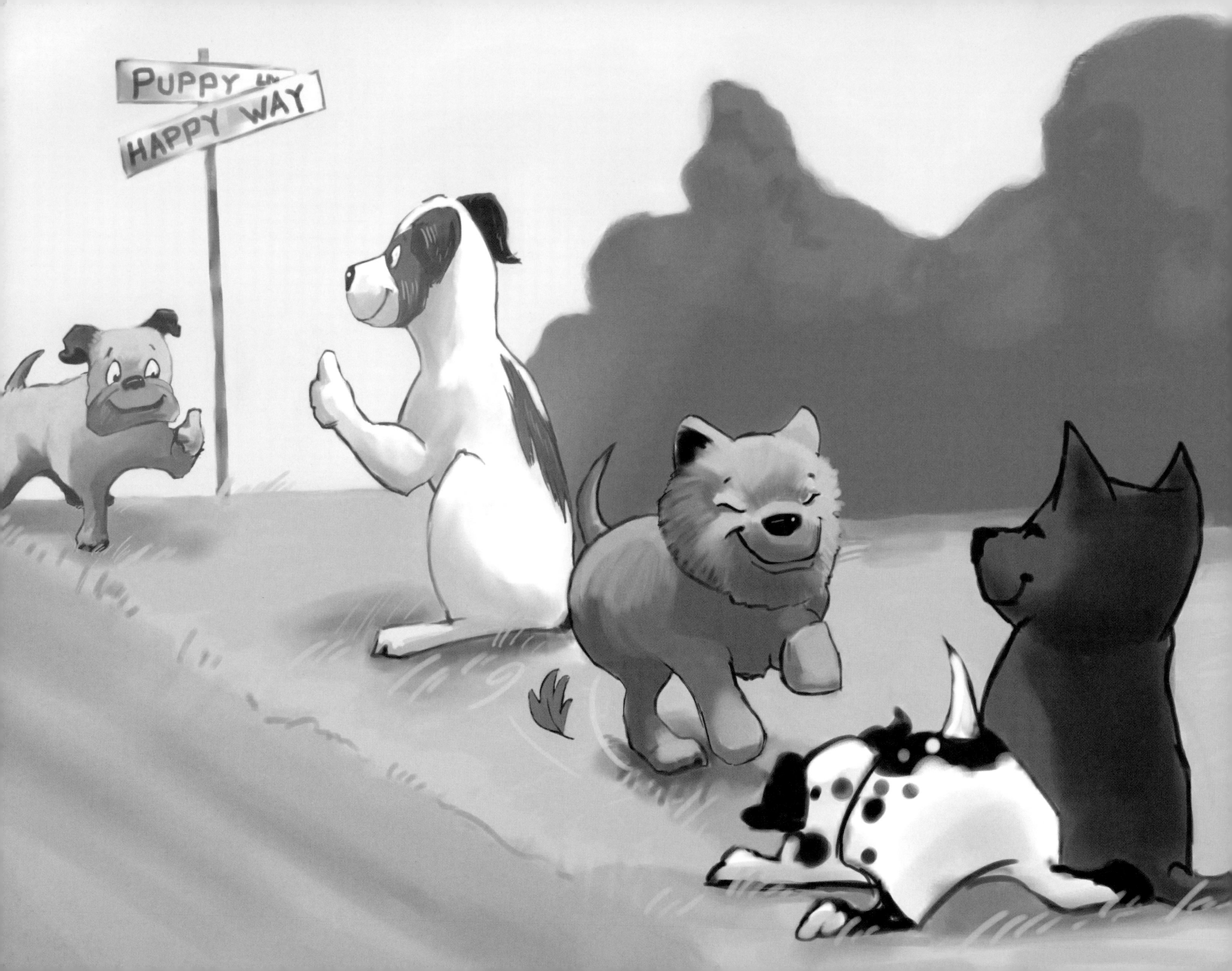
PUPPY
HAPPY WAY

As you are breathing, say, 'in' for each breath in and 'out' for each breath out, then after you count ten breaths in and out, repeat these words,

"I will not chase my tail today.
I will not chase it any day.
I'll use my time for friends and fun,
to hop and skip and play and run.
I will not waste another day.
I'd rather use my time to play."

A very special thanks to the following people (my Dream Catchers), who believed in Max while he was just a dream. Also, to my amazing mother-in-law, Mrs. Carolyn F. Lee (a.k.a. Momma Lee), thank you from the bottom of my heart for not only believing in my dream, but for carrying us both until we were able to fly! I could not have reached this goal without your love, encouragement, and support.

My Dream Catchers:

Allen, Cedric	Greene, Isha	McConico, Kira
Avalos, Natalie	Griffin, Roselind	McDaniel, Debra
Balaban, Naomi	Hairson, Dominique	Miko, Ries
Beck, Torrance	Hardy, Krista	NeSmith, Ethel
Bell, Alana	Hicks, Robin	Nobles, Joy
Boyd, Charlie	Hunter, Karen	Nutman, Kaye
Brice, Malik	Hurst, Heidi	Page- Williams, Tamicha
Carillo, Nancy	Kaahu, Lay	Pender, Timothy
Carlson, Judy	Katsura, Stewart	Pounds-Lewis, Carolyn
Cavor, Althea	Keith, Marcella	Proctor, Tresa
Charles, Robert	King, Jacquelynn	Raciti, Sonja
Doss, Iran	Lee, Carolyn	Reid-Williamson, Lisa
Doss, Mavis	Lee, Denise Ann	Reniva, Rachel
Doss, Robert	Lee, Jessica	Rodriguez, Jaime
Floyd, Donna	Lee, Melissa	Smith, Danyelle
Fullum, Ellen Bodota	Lee, Trefus	Smith, Florenza
Gaddis, Almeda	Lowry, Joshua	Smith, Patrice
Gilliard, Debbie	Lyann, Tiffany	Thomas, Derek
Goodall, Glenda Nakamura	Magnusen, Kay	Washington, Emily
Green, Carolyn	May, Shawnte	Watson, Mary
	Mays, Elaine	